CHINA

by Annie Qaiser

The Child's World®

Published by The Child's World®
1980 Lookout Drive • Mankato, MN 56003-1705
800-599-READ • www.childsworld.com

Acknowledgments
The Child's World®: Mary Berendes, Publishing Director
Red Line Editorial: Editorial direction
The Design Lab: Design
Amnet: Production

Design elements: Shutterstock Images; iStock/Thinkstock
Photographs ©: Shutterstock Images, cover (left top), cover (left
bottom), cover (right), 1 (top), 1 (bottom right), 11, 12, 13, 15
(right), 16–17, 18, 22, 24, 26, 30; iStock/Thinkstock, cover (left
center), 1 (bottom left), 15 (left); Hung Chung Chih/Shutterstock
Images, 5; Collins Chin/iStockphoto, 6–7; Galyna Andrushko/
Shutterstock Images, 8; iStockphoto, 10, 21, 28, 29; Rich Vintage/
iStockphoto, 20; Ariadna de Raadt/Shutterstock Images, 23; Xi Xin
Xing/iStockphoto, 25, 27

ISBN 9781634070409
LCCN 2014959726

Printed in the United States of America
Mankato, MN
July, 2015
PA02268

ABOUT THE AUTHOR

Annie Qaiser loves to read, write, and paint. She lives in the United States with her family. Qaiser's kids are learning Mandarin Chinese!

TABLE OF CONTENTS

CHAPTER 1
WELCOME TO CHINA! 5

CHAPTER 2
THE LAND 8

CHAPTER 3
GOVERNMENT AND CITIES 13

CHAPTER 4
PEOPLE AND CULTURES 20

CHAPTER 5
DAILY LIFE 24

FAST FACTS, 30

GLOSSARY, 31

TO LEARN MORE, 32

INDEX, 32

ARCTIC
OCEAN

ATLANTIC
OCEAN

CHINA

PACIFIC
OCEAN

PACIFIC
OCEAN

INDIAN
OCEAN

SCALE

0   1000 Miles

0   1000 KM

N
W   E
S

SOUTHERN
OCEAN

China covers
3,705,407 square miles
(9,596,960 sq km).
This makes it the
fourth-largest
country in the world.
Only Russia, Canada,
and the United States
are larger.

FUN FACT

ONE WORLD · MANY COUNTRIES

CHAPTER 1

WELCOME TO CHINA!

It is the first day of the Chinese New Year. Beijing's streets are brimming with noise, lights, and people. Red paper decorations hang on doors and windows for good luck. A giant half-dragon, half-lion puppet winds its way down the street!

This creature is called Nian. According to legend, Nian would come down from the mountains during the New Year. To scare Nian, people made loud noises, lit lanterns, and wore the color

People perform the dragon and lion dance during the Chinese New Year celebration in Beijing, China, in 2013.

red. The Chinese still follow these New Year's traditions today.

The Chinese New Year lasts for 15 days. It usually happens in January or February. The exact date depends on the **lunar** calendar.

People follow other New Year's traditions, too. They clean their homes to remove any bad luck before the year begins. Families go to temples. There, they pray for success, happiness, and wealth. Children receive gifts of money in red and gold paper envelopes.

On the last day of the New Year, Chinese families have a large meal. Before they

eat, people put paper strips over their doors. They believe this stops evil from entering their homes. At the meal, people eat foods such as fish, noodles, dumplings, and sweet rice balls.

These Chinese traditions are ancient, but they are still part of modern China. Today, China is a world leader. It has strong businesses and many natural resources that make it a powerful country. Its people are working hard to continue their success.

On the last day of the Chinese New Year, people celebrate by setting out lanterns.

CHAPTER 2

THE LAND

Mount Everest is 29,029 feet (8,848 m) tall. In 1953, mountain climbers reached the top for the first time.

China is the largest country in Asia. Along its eastern and southern borders, China has 8,700 miles (14,000 km) of coast. In the east, China borders the Yellow Sea and the East China Sea. The South China Sea splashes on China's southern border.

China borders 14 countries. Mongolia, Russia, and North Korea are north of China. To the south, China borders Vietnam, Laos, Myanmar, India, Bhutan, and Nepal. In the west, China's neighbors are Pakistan, Afghanistan, Tajikistan, Kyrgyzstan, and Kazakhstan.

Mountains tower over many parts of China. The Himalayas are China's largest mountain range. They are in southwestern China. The Himalayas have steep, jagged peaks. One of the peaks is called is Mount Everest. It is the world's highest point. Mount Everest rises on the border of China and Nepal.

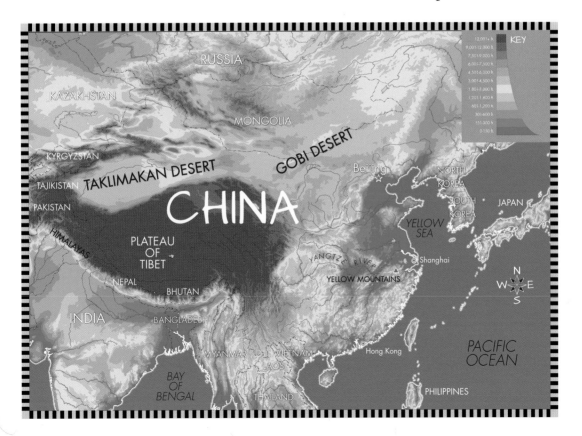

The Yellow Mountain range is in eastern China. It is an area of great beauty. Pine trees grow there. Streams and waterfalls splash down the sides of the mountains. Unusually shaped rocks rise from the ground. Mist and clouds often cover the rocks and mountains.

China also has plains. They are flat areas with rich soil. Many of China's farms are on the plains. Crops such as rice, wheat, peanuts, and cotton grow well there. The plains also

The Yellow Mountains are known as the Huangshan in Chinese. Mists rise over Huangshan 250 days each year.

have lots of grass for farm animals to eat. Most of China's plains are in the eastern part of the country.

China also has deserts. The Gobi Desert stretches out between China and Mongolia. It covers about 500,000 square miles (1.3 million sq km). Most of the Gobi desert is rock. The Taklimakan Desert is also in China. It is one of the largest sandy deserts in the world.

China's most important river is the Yangtze. It begins high in the mountains of southwestern China. It flows east and then drains into the Yellow Sea. The land in the Yangtze **delta** is

The Yangtze River flows for 3,915 miles (6,300 km). It is the longest river in Asia.

rich in natural resources. Iron, copper, gold, and oil can be found there.

Monsoons affect the weather in China. Monsoons are strong winds. In the summer, the monsoons bring heavy rains. In the winter, monsoons blow cold, dry air across China. In the Gobi Desert, the winds can create dust storms.

FUN FACT • ONE WORLD • MANY COUNTRIES

The Silk Road was an ancient trail that connected China to Europe. It allowed people to trade goods such as silk, gold, silver, and wool. Camels often carried the trade goods.

CHAPTER 3

GOVERNMENT AND CITIES

China's Great Hall of the People is where lawmakers meet to pass laws.

China's official name is the People's Republic of China. It has 22 provinces. A province is similar to a state. China also has

five regions. They are part of China, but they have more power
to govern themselves.

China has a communist government. In this system, the
government controls most parts of the country. It owns the
factories, farms, and businesses. In exchange, people receive

many services from the government. These services include free schools and clinics.

The leaders in China are all members of the Communist party. The premier is the leader of China's government. The National People's Congress is the group of people who make China's laws. The People's Court makes sure the laws are followed.

China's government meets in Beijing. It is China's capital. Almost 16 million people live there. Beijing is an ancient city. People have been living there for nearly 2,000 years. It has many historic areas. The best known is the Forbidden City.

China's currency

China's flag

The Forbidden City is a group of buildings used by emperors since the 1420s. A strong wall surrounded the buildings. Only the emperor, his family, and government officials could enter. The Forbidden City remained the center of Chinese power for 500 years.

Shanghai is southeast of Beijing. Shanghai is China's largest city. More than 20 million people live there. Shanghai is along the East China Sea and the Yangtze River. This location has made it a busy port city. Ships bring goods into and out of China there.

Many businesses and factories are based in

Shanghai. It is China's leading industrial city. Businesses in Shanghai make a variety of goods. They include items such as clothing, electronics, and hardware.

Hong Kong is another important city. Beginning in 1842, England ruled Hong Kong. In 1997, Hong Kong became part of China again. Today, it has a mix of English and Chinese culture. Hong Kong is known as one of the world's best cities for shopping. It is also an important city for business.

Today, the Forbidden City is open to visitors. Its buildings are excellent examples of early Chinese architecture.

China's businesses are growing quickly. They make goods and provide services that people in other countries like. This has made China the world's largest **exporter**. China's major trading partners are the United States, Japan, and South Korea.

The Great Wall of China is one of the world's largest building projects. Emperors began building it in the seventh century BC. The wall protected China from invaders to the north. Today, 3,900 miles (6,276 km) of the wall still stand.

FUN FACT

ONE WORLD · MANY COUNTRIES

GLOBAL CONNECTIONS

China has the world's second-largest economy, after the United States. Recently, China has become the largest manufacturing country. China makes everything from toys, shoes, and clothes to televisions, computers, and cars.

China also exports more than any other country in the world. It sells most of the products to different countries. The more products China sells, the more money comes back to China. This money helps China become more powerful.

The United States, Japan, South Korea, and a few European countries buy most of the products made in China. These countries are China's top export partners. Many of the things people use daily are made in China.

CHAPTER 4

PEOPLE AND CULTURES

Many Chinese families are small. The government discourages families from having more than one or two children.

China is a **diverse** country. More than 1.3 billion people live there. It is the world's most populated country.

China's people belong to many different **ethnic** groups. About 92 percent of Chinese people are Han. Han is China's largest ethnic group. The rest of China is made up of 55 **minority** groups. The Zhuang are the biggest minority group.

In China, people speak Mandarin Chinese. It is also known as *putonghua*, which means "common language." There are many other Chinese **dialects** spoken in the country. They include Cantonese and Shanghainese.

China is officially an **atheist** country. People are only allowed to practice some religions. Buddhism is the largest religion in China. People also practice religions such as Christianity, Islam,

Two women pray in the Grand Hall of the Jade Buddha Temple in Shanghai, China. The Buddhist temple was founded in 1882.

and Taoism. Taoism is a religion that began in China. It focuses on the role of nature and the universe in a person's life.

China is considered to be a country of inventors. The Chinese were the first to create paper, the compass, gunpowder, and printing. These items are often called the Four Great Inventions.

The arts also have a long history in China. Calligraphy is China's oldest art. Calligraphers write the dots and lines of letters in an artistic way. Their tools are ink, a brush, and paper. Calligraphers study for many years to perfect their styles.

Festivals are important in China, too. One of these is the Dragon Boat Festival. It falls on the fifth day of the fifth month on the lunar calendar. At the festival, people race boats that have a dragon's head painted on the front. People also eat

Two teams compete at a dragon boat race in Foshan City, China.

zongzi. It is sticky rice stuffed with sweet and salty fillings, and wrapped in bamboo leaves or reeds.

The Qingming Festival celebrates the beginning of spring. Family members offer gifts and make sacrifices for their loved ones who have died. They clean the graves of their loved ones. They also burn **incense** to ward off evil spirits.

FUN FACT

ONE WORLD · MANY COUNTRIES

Chinese names are written in an order that is different than in English. Chinese names begin with the last name and then end with the first name. For example, a person named Will Johnson would write his name as Johnson Will in China.

CHAPTER 5

DAILY LIFE

When Chinese children grow up, they are expected to take care of their parents and grandparents.

The Chinese culture values family and respect for elders. Many people live with their relatives. Grandparents often live with their son's family. Children grow up seeing their mother and father caring for their parents.

A Chinese family enjoys a meal together. In China, people usually eat with chopsticks rather than forks.

Families often eat meals together. Each region has a special food. One of the most famous dishes comes from Beijing. It is Peking duck. The duck is roasted until the meat is tender and the skin is crispy. Most meals also include rice, noodles, and vegetables.

People in China often wear clothing similar to that worn in the United States. Sometimes they wear traditional clothing. For women, traditional clothes are called a *cheongsam*. It began as

The cheongsam has a high collar and fastens in the front.

a long, loose dress made of cotton or silk. Over time, the dress became shorter and more fitted.

Another type of traditional clothing is a Tang jacket. It is a long, loose jacket. It fastens down the front. The fasteners are braided trim with buttons. The jacket has a high collar and pockets. Men or women can wear the Tang jacket.

Homes in China come in many styles. Traditional Chinese homes face south. This allows the sun to warm the houses.

A family wears traditional Tang jackets.

Courtyards are in the center of a traditional home. The rooms in the home surround the courtyard.

In rural areas, people often live in huts with straw roofs. These homes may have dirt floors. Kitchens and bathrooms are outdoors, far from the main living area. Fires made from coal are used to heat homes and cook meals. To get clean water, people often have to walk long distances to wells.

In cities, many people live in tall apartment buildings. City homes have modern appliances such as stoves, refrigerators, and washing machines. Dishwashers and dryers are not common. They are considered luxuries.

People in Shanghai ride bicycles and motorbikes to get from place to place.

The transportation system in China has changed in recent years. People in China can get around by plane, car, subway, and train. People also use bicycles or walk. Bullet trains with speeds up to 200 miles (322 km) per hour connect main cities.

While bullet trains are modern, many parts of life in China are still traditional. Chinese people are proud of their history. Their creations and inventions have shaped the world. Today, China's people continue to work hard. They have made their country a world leader with a bright future.

DAILY LIFE FOR CHILDREN

The education system in China is very competitive. Children have to study hard and take many exams from a young age to get into a good school.

A Chinese elementary school student's typical day begins at 8:00 in the morning. Students take challenging courses such as physics, chemistry, and biology. The day ends at 5:00 in the evening. In the evenings, students do homework and study.

Rat	Ox	Tiger	Rabbit
Dragon	Snake	Horse	Goat
Monkey	Rooster	Dog	Pig

FUN FACT

ONE WORLD • MANY COUNTRIES

Each year in the Chinese calendar is connected with one of 12 animals. They are the rat, ox, tiger, rabbit, dragon, snake, horse, goat, monkey, rooster, dog, and pig. Many people believe a person will take on the traits of the animal from the year of their birth.

FAST FACTS

Population: 1.3 billion

Area: 3,705,407 square miles (9,596,960 sq km)

Capital: Beijing

Largest Cities: Beijing, Shanghai, and Guangzhou

Form of Government: Communist State

Trading Partners: The United States, Japan, and South Korea

Major Holidays: Chinese New Year, Dragon Boat Festival, and Qingming Festival

National Dish: Peking Duck (roasted duck that is famous for its crispy skin)

Chinese children hold up the envelopes filled with money they received during the Chinese New Year.

GLOSSARY

atheist (AY-thee-ist) To be atheist is to not believe that God exists. An atheist government does not have an official religion.

delta (DEL-tuh) A delta is an area of land made of sand and mud near the mouth of a river. Many people live in the Yangtze delta.

dialects (DYE-uh-lekts) Dialects are unique forms of a language particular to certain places or groups of people. Chinese people speak many dialects.

diverse (dye-VURS) To be diverse is to be varied or assorted. China has a diverse population.

ethnic (ETH-nik) An ethnic group has a common language, culture, or religion. China has many ethnic groups.

exporter (EX-sport-er) An exporter is a person, business, or country that sells goods to other countries. China is the world's largest exporter.

incense (IN-sense) Incense is a material that produces a pleasant scent when burned. People burn incense as a form of prayer.

lunar (LOO-nuhr) Lunar describes something relating to the moon or its cycles. Chinese festivals are based on lunar dates.

minority (muh-NOR-uh-tee) A minority is a smaller group of people of a certain race, ethnicity, or religion that lives among a larger group within a country. Some Chinese people come from different minority groups.

To Learn More

BOOKS

Chen, Haiyan. *Eight Dragons on the Roof and Other Tales*. South San Francisco: China Books, 2012.

Mah, Adeline Yen. *China: Land of Dragons and Emperors*. New York: Delacorte Press, 2009.

Wang, Qicheng. *The Big Book of China*. San Francisco: Long River Press, 2010.

WEB SITES

Visit our Web site for links about China: childsworld.com/links

Note to Parents, Teachers, and Librarians: We routinely verify our Web links to make sure they are safe and active sites. So encourage your readers to check them out!

Index

Beijing, 15, 25

calligraphy, 22
climate, 12
clothing, 25–26

economy, 18–19

food, 22–23, 25
Four Great Inventions, 22

Gobi Desert, 11–12

Himalayas, 9
holidays, 5–7, 22–23
homes, 26–27

religion, 21–22

schools, 29
Shanghai, 16–17

Taklimakan Desert, 11
transportation, 28

Yangtze River, 11, 16
Yellow Mountains, 10